LIFE SKILLS
IN THE PACIFIC

Basic Gardening

Stephen Potek

OXFORD

Contents

Introduction

Basic Gardening is about how to set up a food garden to grow food for the family, as well as selling excess food at the market. It contains instructions on how to prepare the garden plot, planting and harvesting methods for major crops, and how to deal with pests and diseases. The last chapter discusses financial management issues; that is, how to make money by growing food in your garden.

This book is written to complement the newly introduced 'Making a Living' subject for upper primary students. It supports the philosophy of Education, which emphasises relevant education and self-reliance. It teaches students useful skills and relevant knowledge to enable them to become useful members of their local communities.

Strand: *Managing Resources*
Sub Strand: *Crop and animal management*
Outcomes: 7.1.3: *explain appropriate crop management and animal husbandry practices and demonstrate these through undertaking a practical project*
8.1.3: *plan, design and implement a crop or animal project suited to local conditions and resources aimed at generating an income*

I encourage all students to take up gardening as it is not only rewarding in nutritional and monetary terms, but also a great form of exercise.

Stephen Potek

Food gardens in Papua New Guinea

Most people in Papua New Guinea live in rural areas, farm for a living and are almost self-sufficient by growing their own food. A food garden will produce a variety of crops that provide a balanced diet to sustain a healthy body. Root and grain crops provide carbohydrates, and fruit and vegetables provide proteins, **vitamins** and minerals.

People **cultivate** food gardens at or near their home to grow crops for the family and to sell in the market. To be a successful food gardener, you need to decide what plant foods to grow, where and when to grow them and how much to grow and harvest. The choice of food grown for the home depends on what types of nutritious foods your family enjoys eating. To decide what crops to grow for sale, you might visit local markets to collect information on what crops are sold there, what people buy, how much they buy and what prices they pay for them at different times.

A checklist for choosing plants for a food garden

- ✓ Only plant crops that grow best in your particular area.
- ✓ Choose plants from each of the three food groups (energy, body building, protective) to provide the family with a balanced diet.
- ✓ Traditional vegetables are better than most introduced vegetables.
- ✓ Legumes are important for good nutrition and good gardens.
- ✓ Fruit and nut trees should be planted for both shade and food.

Planning a food garden

When you are planning a food garden, it is important to choose an area that is quite flat and not too muddy. If possible, choose an area near a water supply to make watering easier in the driest part of the year. Well-drained **loam** (rich soil) is best, but bad soil can be improved.

Clearing the site

Bush vegetation must be cleared very carefully. Fruit and nut trees should be left on the site as they will supply shade as well as food, and can help prevent soil **erosion**. The **topsoil** needs to be tilled with a digging fork or stick to remove all **roots**. Once the area has been cleared, it can be burned but only lightly so that **nutrients** stay in the ground. The dry leaves and rotting tree matter should be left and turned over in the soil to add nutrients. Some ground-covering plants – such as aupa, pawpaw, pumpkin and beans – can be planted immediately on cleared areas to help maintain nutrients and prevent soil erosion as well as produce food. This also reduces the amount of weeding required.

Designing the layout

When the garden area has been cleared, you can dig the ground and make **mounds** or **ridges**. If the garden is on a slope, the ridges should be made across the slope, not down it. This will stop the loss of good soil during heavy rain and will hold water in the garden during the dry season. Ridges and mounds also allow water to drain through the soil, so that the plant roots do not become waterlogged.

The layout of the garden depends on what suits you best. Remember that you should be able to reach the centre of a plot with your hands when you stand on a path; otherwise, you might have to step on it to remove **weeds**, fertilise or water the plants in the middle, and this can damage the plants. The length of the plots will depend on the number of different crops you want to grow, and the size of the available land.

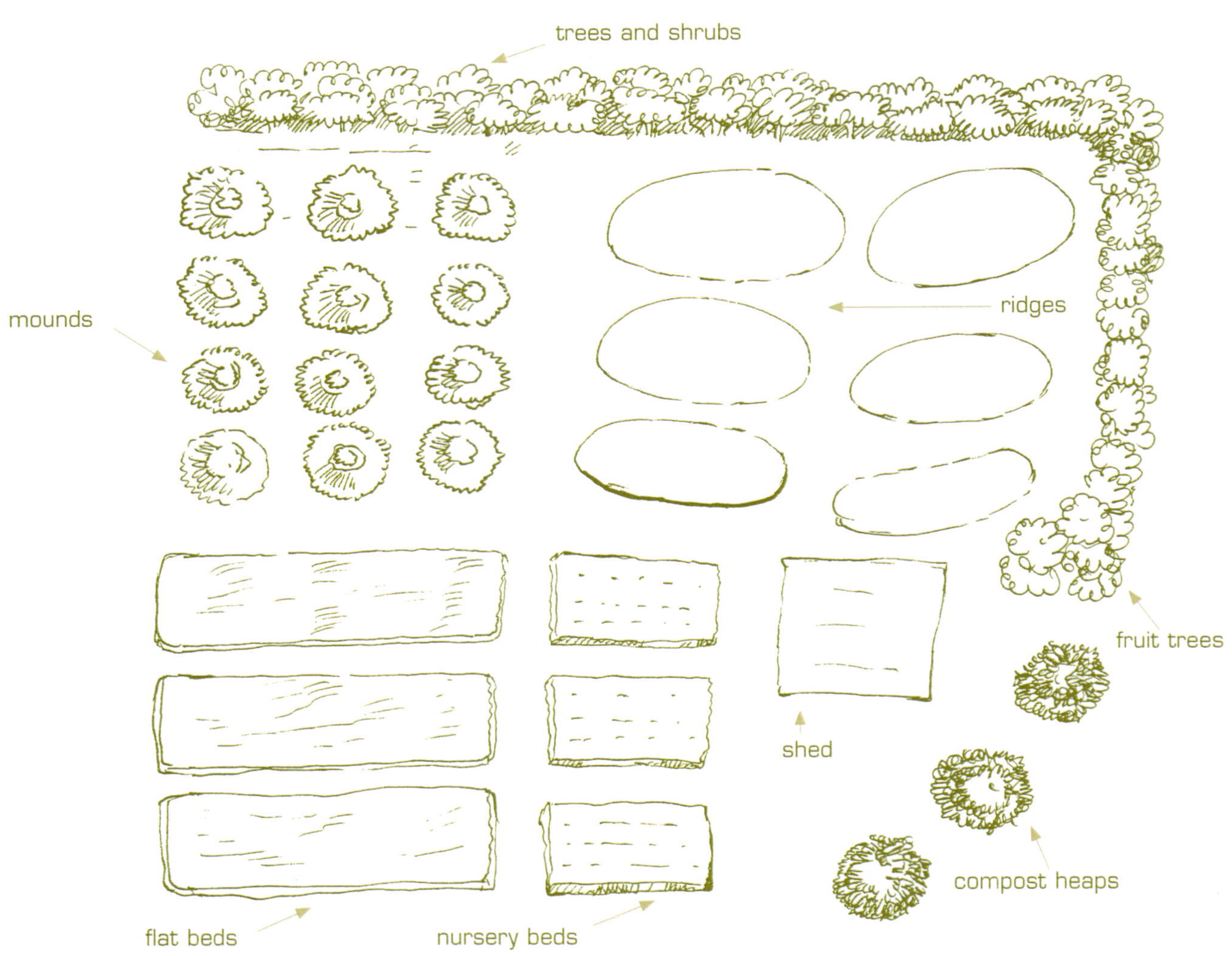

A bird's eye view of a garden on part flat and part sloping land

Garden tools

A tool is something that makes work easier. There are many jobs to be done when growing vegetables, and different tools are used for different jobs. Basic garden tools are sold in stores. If possible, buy good quality tools that will last a long time and look after them well. Basic tools may include a digging stick, a bush knife, a **spade**, a fork, a steel axe, a rake, a hoe, a watering can, string and a bucket. Other useful tools include secateurs, a hand fork, a hand spade, a tape measure, a cutlass and a wheelbarrow.

Digging stick

Bush knife

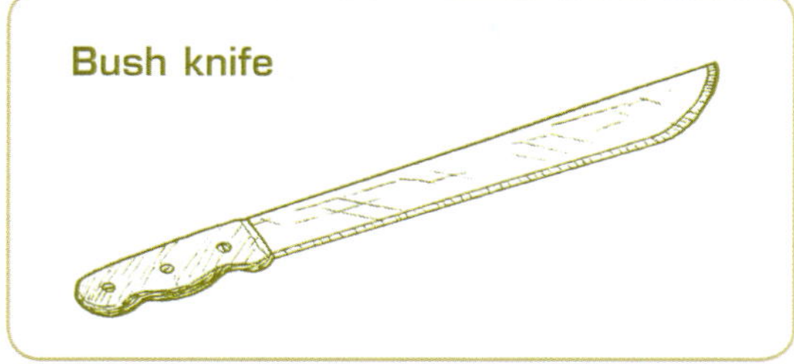

Spade

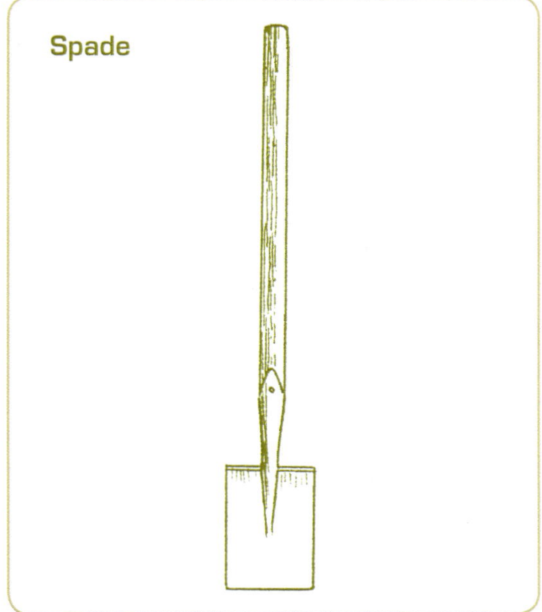

Fork

Steel axe

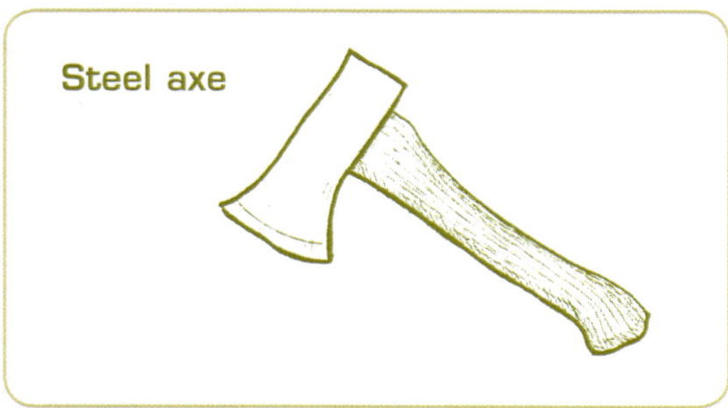

Secateurs

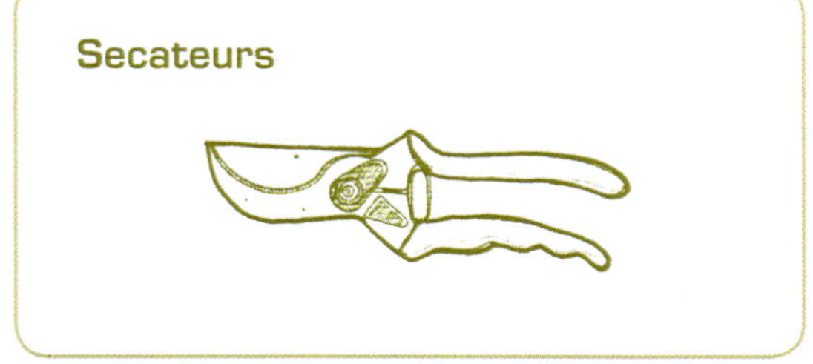

Hand fork

Rake

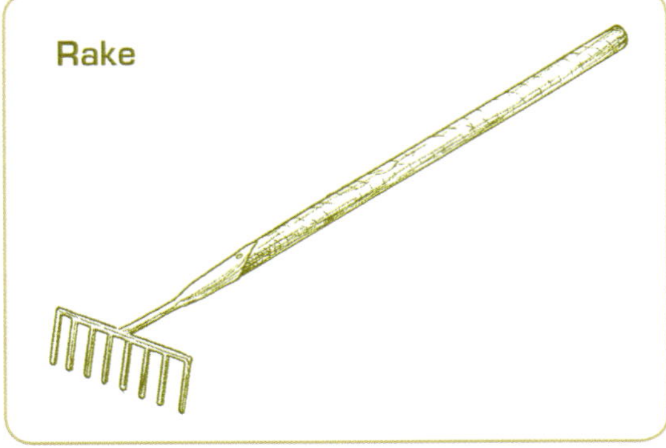

Hoe

Bucket

Watering can

String

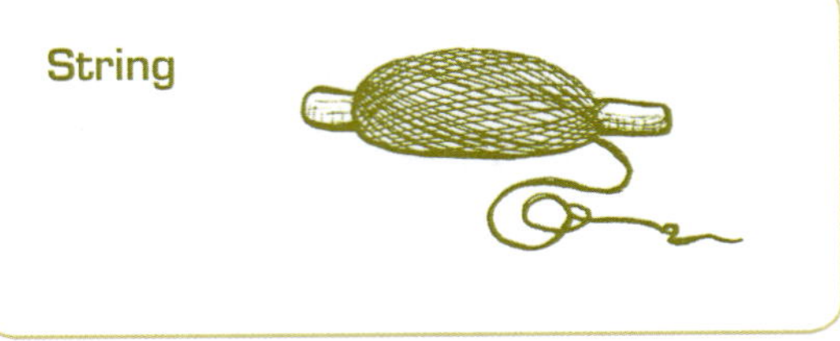

Hand spade

Tape measure

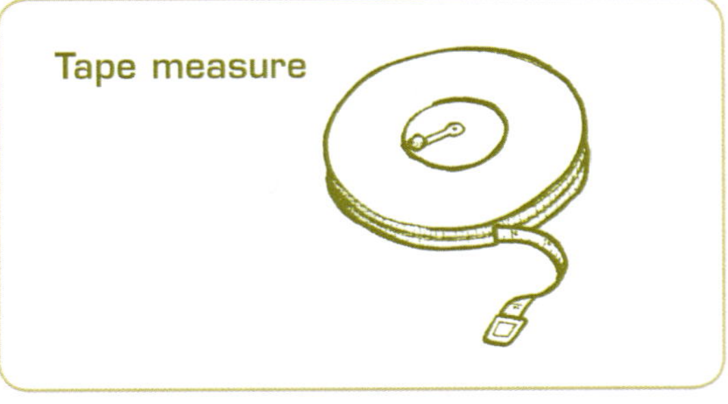

Wheelbarrow

Garden preparation

Soil

Good soil is essential for plant growth. If we take nutrients from the soil by growing plants in it, and do not return nutrients, soon the soil will have nothing to give to the plants. Nutrients are also lost through soil erosion so it is important to add **organic matter** to keep the soil **fertile**. Soil must be prepared with the right type of nutrients so that healthy plants can grow and produce a maximum **yield**. The quickest and most efficient way of keeping soil fertile is to ensure it is rich in organic matter. This will:

- give plants nutrients
- help keep the soil together
- help hold water in the soil
- add living **organisms** to the soil to help rot dead plants and animals.

A good gardener puts large amounts of organic matter, or **compost**, into the soil to make it fertile and keep a good soil structure. Compost is made up of **manure** from farm animals and rotted plant and animal material. It has all the elements that plants need to grow well. When the compost has decomposed completely, it is called **humus**. Humus has all the nutrients that growing plants need to grow well and produce a good yield.

How to make a compost heap

- Select a site away from the house but near the garden, and where water doesn't form puddles during the rainy season.
- Mark a space 1m by 1m or slightly larger.
- Stake the edges of the space with sticks to hold the compost in place.
- Collect green and dry leaves, soft **stems**, kitchen waste, garden refuse, grass and manure.

STEPS

1. Use corn stalks or non-woody plant material as a base.
2. Make a pile of dry green leaves on the base, about 15-30cm deep.
3. Add a handful of **fertiliser** containing nitrogen, to help **bacteria** to multiply.
4. Sprinkle it with water.
5. Add a thin layer of manure or old compost and sprinkle it with water to start **decomposition**.
6. Add 5cm of soil.
7. Repeat steps 1-6 until the heap is about 1m high.
8. Cover the heap with dry grass or broad leaves to keep it dry.

How to make a compost heap *continued …*

- After three months the compost can be added to the garden soil.
- Build three heaps one or two months apart to make sure that compost is always available.
- The older the compost heap, the better the decomposition and the better the nutrients are for the soil and plants.
- If there is no rain, compost heaps should be watered lightly so they don't dry up.
- Use one spade of compost per square metre of soil and mix it in well to prevent nutrients from being washed away by rain.

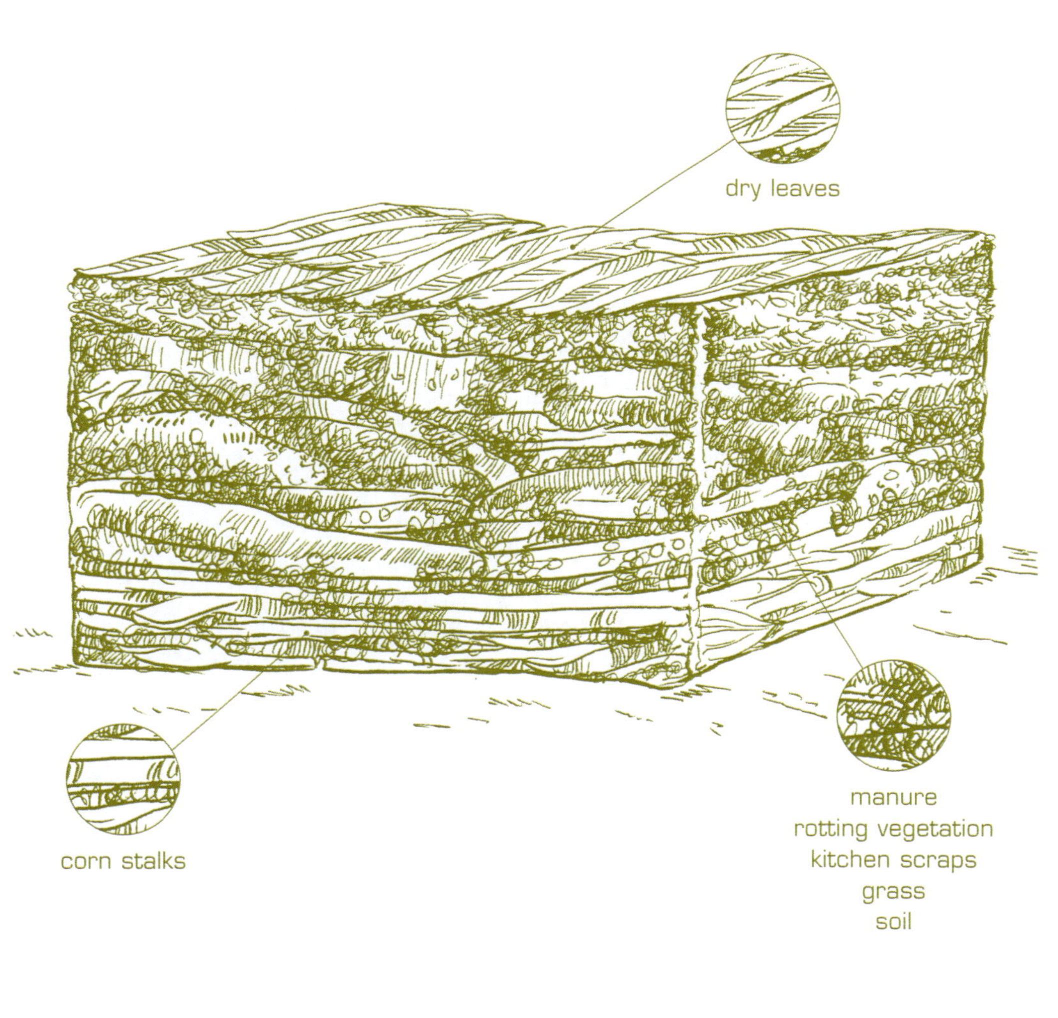

Garden plots

Garden plots can be rectangular, square or circular. They can be raised above the ground, made level with the ground or sunk into the ground.

Raised plots

Raised garden plots are widely used in areas of high rainfall, heavy soil and poor **drainage**. Raising the plot above the ground surface improves drainage and ensures that crops are not flooded during heavy rain. Paths are marked between the plots and act as natural drainage channels in wet weather.

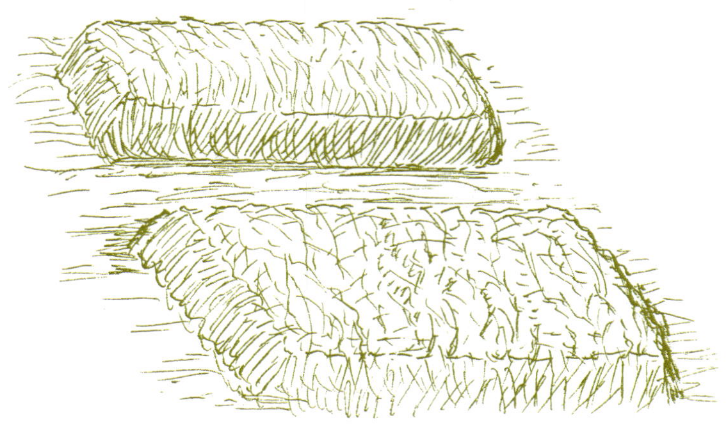

Flat plots

Most flat gardens have rectangular plots. Leave a path of 60 to 90 centimetres around groups of plots to allow space for your wheelbarrow when applying compost or during harvest. If the garden is on a slope, plots should be raised across the slope, not down it, to minimise soil erosion. Soil retaining walls should be built on the sloping side of the plot.

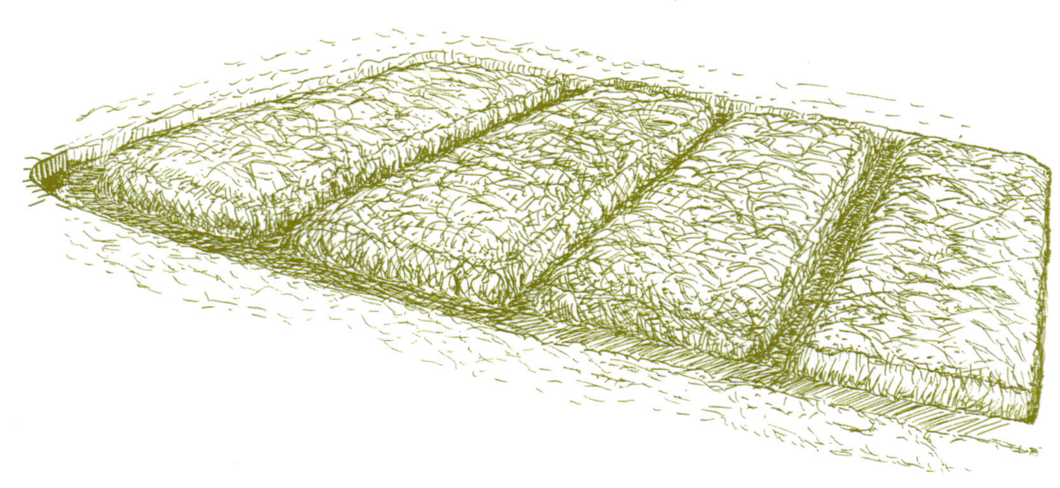

Ridges
A ridge is one long continuous garden plot.

Mounds
A mound is soil collected into a circular raised heap. Mounds can be different shapes and sizes depending on the crop grown. Mounds can be staggered so that water running down the slope will go around the mounds.

Sunken plots
Sunken plots can be any shape and will allow water to drain slowly to the roots in areas that have a long dry season. Sunken plots are flat areas with soil at the sides to keep water from running off. The soil at the sides can be taken from the paths.

Making garden plots

STEPS

1

Loosen the soil and remove any weeds and large stones.

2

Add compost to the plot and dig the soil until they are well mixed. Try to dig a spade deep – about 30cm. Start at one end and dig a trench about 30cm wide across the plot. Each time you dig, turn over the soil at the top. Work in straight lines across the plot.

3

Break large pieces of soil into small pieces until the soil becomes smooth, then use your rake to level the plot. Make a small ridge at the edge of the plot to help control soil erosion by stopping water running off during heavy rain.

Planting seeds and seedlings

Seeds such as corn, beans and peanuts can be planted directly in garden plots. Other plants, especially introduced vegetables, need to be grown in **seed beds**. You can **transplant** the **seedlings** into garden plots once they are established. Seedlings can be grown in ridges or mounds, or in raised or flat garden plots. They need to be transplanted in good soil and watered before and after transplanting.

Seed selection

Local seeds are more reliable than imported seeds. Select only healthy seeds for maximum yield. Growing your own seeds also has many advantages:

- you can select seeds to meet your own needs
- you know the parent plants that the seeds come from
- you can choose seeds from plants which grow well under specific soil and climatic conditions.

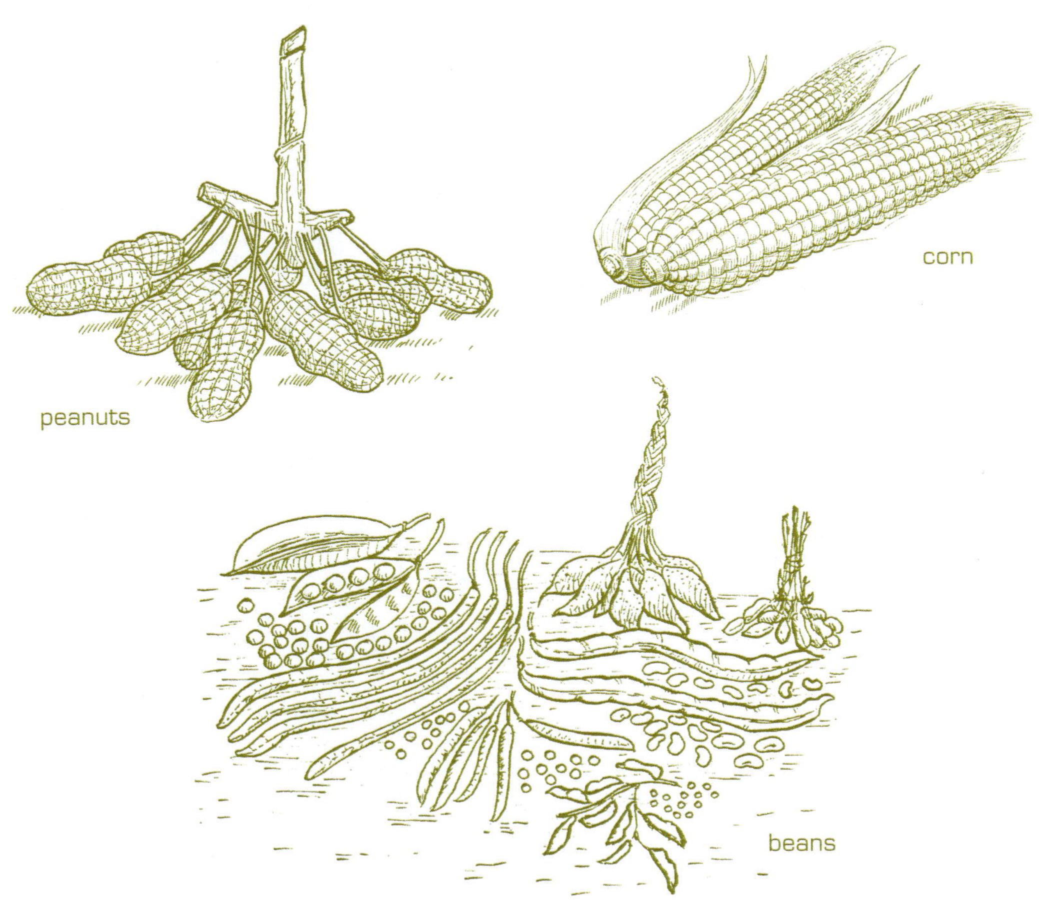

Preparing a seed bed

- Prepare the seed bed, no more than 1m wide, in a sunny place that can be shaded.
- Add a little manure and dig the soil until it is smooth.
- Build the seed bed a little higher than the ground so that water can drain away.

HOW TO SOW THE SEEDS

1. Place the seeds in rows across the seed bed.

2. Cover them with the fine soil and water carefully.

3. Put **mulch** over the seeds until they grow.

Transplanting seedlings

Seedlings grown in a seed bed need to be removed and planted in the garden plot. This is called transplanting. It is done when the seedlings are ten to 15 centimetres tall. Be careful not to damage the young seedlings when you are transplanting. It is best to transplant on cloudy days, early in the morning or late in the afternoon, to prevent seedlings drying out and dying.

HOW TO TRANSPLANT SEEDLINGS

1. Water the seedlings in the seed bed.

2. Mark out the rows and dig planting holes in the garden plot. Make sure they are deep and wide enough.

3. Add a little manure and mix it well with the soil so that it does not burn the roots of young seedlings.

4. Fill the planting holes with water. The water will drain away, leaving the soil wet.

Transplanting seedlings *continued …*

5

Use a flat stick or trowel to carry the seedlings to the plot, keeping the soil around the roots. Transplant just a few seedlings each time to prevent them drying out.

6

Plant each seedling fairly deep in its own hole, with the bottom leaves at ground level. Press the soil down around the seedling.

7

Water the seedlings after transplanting.

Staking

Plants such as tomatoes, climbing beans and yams that have weak stems, or are climbers, must be staked to ensure more fruit is produced and the plant is not damaged. To stake climbing plants, firmly place sticks in ridges, between the plants, which slant towards each other where the sticks meet. Tie plant stems to the stalk, using string or vines, as the plant grows.

Weeding

A weed is a plant that grows even though it wasn't planted. Weeds take nutrients out of the soil so if there are a lot of weeds in your garden, your vegetables will compete with them for nutrients and won't grow well. Remove the weeds before they are well established but take care not to damage the roots of the vegetables. Use a hoe or hand fork for this job.

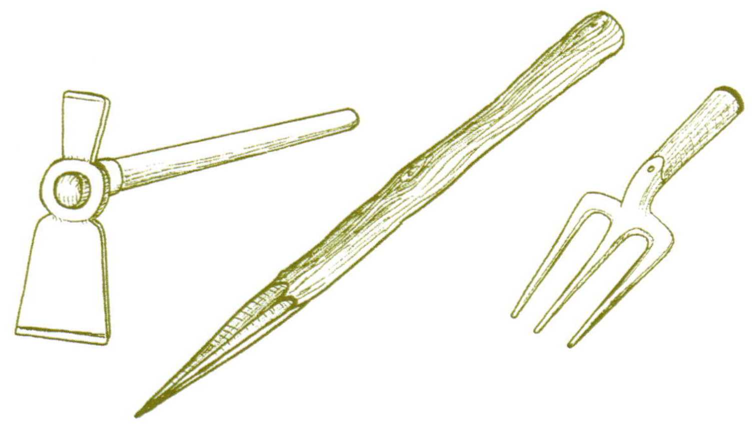

Mulching

Mulch is a layer of materials that is put over the topsoil. Mulch:

- stops the soil from drying out
- stops erosion by keeping soil from being washed away
- stops weeds growing
- adds fertility to the soil.

Mulch applied at an early stage will help control weeds. Applying fertiliser or manure to growing plants is called 'top dressing'. This is done to help the vegetables grow better; however, fertilisers can be expensive to purchase.

Pest and weed control

Insects and disease can damage and kill plants. If pests and plant diseases are not controlled, they can damage a whole field of crops in a short time. In the tropics, temperature and humidity are ideal all year round for insects, bacteria, **fungi** and **viruses** to live. Pests and diseases can eat or destroy more crops in the field and in **storage** than people eat, and weak plants are very easily damaged by **disease organisms**.

Colour change in leaves
When spots on the leaves turn white, it may be caused by a fungus disease called **mildew**, which is very common in the tropics. It may also be caused by diseased roots which are no longer able to take in nutrients. When the whole leaf begins to change colour, check the roots to make sure they are healthy.

Holes in the leaves
The appearance of many small holes in the leaf is a sign of disease. If a fungus or bacteria is attacking the plant, the leaf tissue begins to change colour, then dies and the tissue falls out leaving holes.

Damping off
This occurs when a fungus causes a plant to wilt, drop its leaves and die very quickly. The fungus can be found in the soil and it can be carried by the wind or infected seed.

Plant parts die
If the roots of potatoes or peanuts die, it is usually caused by fungus or bacterial organisms.

Change in plant organs
Sometimes the whole ear of a corn plant becomes covered with a grey or white fungus. Inside the skin is a black powder which is a fungus called 'smut'. In some cocoa trees in coastal areas, many of the fruits do not mature but turn brown and die young. Later they become small black dried-up fruit called 'mummies'.

Rotting tissue
Green stems and softer wood stems, roots, leaves, buds and fruits may rot away or become watery and soft. Most of these rots are caused by fungi. In large areas, fungi can be treated by using chemicals called 'fungicides', but in a small garden it is best to control by weeding and avoid over-watering because fungi multiply in moist, weedy conditions.

Common pests and treatments

Pest/disease	Description	Plant damage	Treatment
Aphids (pest)	Small green or black sucking insects usually found in large numbers	Attack leaves and stems of vegetables but cause most damage to cabbages Slow plant growth	Wash off with water Homemade pesticide: derris, pyrethrum Spray with malathion 95% WP 10g in 5l water Ladybirds also control aphids
Beetles (pest)	Chewing insects	Feed on vegetables and large numbers can destroy all the leaves of the plant Also eat flowers	Control weeds when the plants are small Pick off by hand and kill Homemade pesticide: pyrethrum
Caterpillars/ Cutworm (pest)	Chewing insects which usually develop from eggs on the underside of leaves Cutworms are found about 5cm under surface of the soil	Feed on foliage and tender stems and they are the most damaging pest in the garden Eat young leaves causing holes to appear Cut seedlings at base	Pick off by hand and kill Homemade pesticide: pyrethrum Spray with Dipterex 95% WP 25g in 5l of water Sprinkle cutworm bait around plant
Slugs and snails (pest)	A type of worm that leaves slimy trails	Feed on plants at night	Control weeds when the plants are young Pick slugs and snails at night and destroy
Nematodes (pest)	Small worms that live in plants causing disease	Roots become swollen and plant growth is stunted, producing low yields	Crop rotation Remove affected plants and burn them Plant another type of crop in that area
Fungi (disease)	Micro-organisms that attack plants and are carried in the air, soil and water	Soft or dry rot Smut appears on corn Dead roots	Fungicides Control weeds Avoid over-watering
Bacteria (disease)	Micro-organisms that attack plants and are carried in the air, soil and water or by insects	Leaves at the base will be brown, dry, twisted and drooping Plants eventually die	Crop rotation Remove affected plants and burn them Plant another type of crop in that area
Virus (disease)	Micro-organisms that attack plants and are carried in the air, soil and water	Rusty spots, powdery mildew, and yellowish pattern on leaves Plants eventually die	Crop rotation Remove affected plants and burn them Plant another type of crop in that area

Cultural control of diseases

Cultural control of diseases means anything that a gardener can do to stop damage from diseases without using expensive chemicals. Recommended methods include:

Seed and plant selection

Choose disease-resistant varieties where possible.

Shifting cultivation

Moving the garden from place to place has the same effect on disease control as crop rotation. Moving to new ground and resting the old garden for many years removes the plants that disease-producing organisms live on, so they can't multiply.

Crop rotation and mixed cropping

Disease-producing organisms have less chance to multiply when one crop is harvested and a different crop is planted after it, and when different crops are grown together.

Correct feeding and watering

Healthy plants are able to resist disease much better than weak plants. The correct use of organic manure and compost will help keep plants healthy. Watering the garden in the morning or early afternoon will give the soil surface a chance to dry out by nightfall. This will reduce the danger of wilt caused by fungus disease.

Destruction of diseased plants

Prune any diseased parts of a plant and burn them. Some plants, like corn infected with corn smut disease, should be burnt immediately. Do not use any seed that comes from diseased plants.

Insect protection

Insects can carry disease to your plants so controlling weeds and keeping insects away from your garden will help control some diseases.

Rubbish removal

Keep your garden clean. All rubbish, diseased vegetables, rotting fruits, stems and leaves should be regularly removed from the garden and burnt.

Climbing plants

Some climbing plants, like beans and cucumber, can be trained to grow on a frame of sticks. This stops them from coming in contact with fungus organisms on the ground.

How disease travels

Air
Wind can carry the tiny **spores** of fungi, bacteria and viruses. They are smaller than dust and can travel long distances.

Water
Rivers can carry disease-producing organisms to areas that were previously disease-free.

Animals
Some disease-producing organisms live in the soil and can be carried on the feet of pigs or the feet and bodies of other animals that rub against soil or plants. Birds can easily carry diseases a long distance on their feet or beaks. Insects move from plant to plant and carry disease organisms on their bodies. Some insects pierce the skins of plants to suck the juices, allowing disease to enter the plant.

Seeds
Seeds can be infected with disease at harvest time. The disease organisms stick onto the seed coat and when the seeds are distributed to other areas, disease is spread.

Plant cuttings
Disease can be carried with taro tops, sweet potato vines, sugar cane stems or any other cuttings that are moved from one garden to another, or further away.

Mulch from diseased plants
Stems, leaves or whole plants used for mulch can be a source of disease. Straw used as packing material and shipped to another country may end up as mulch in a garden somewhere and introduce disease organisms.

Compost from diseased plants
Some disease organisms may not be destroyed in the heat of the compost heap. When it is spread on the garden, the new plants growing there may become diseased.

Tools
Tools can carry disease and infect the garden, so it's important to keep them clean. You can even spread disease with a knife when you cut the **corms** of a diseased taro and then cut the corms of a healthy one.

Selection of food plants

Choosing crops

Traditional food crops are easy to grow, very nutritious and relatively disease-free. You should plant crops every one or two months so there will always be some foods ready for harvest all year round. This will help to prevent food shortages and wastage.

Important traditional foods include aibika, aupa, ferns, and karakap (much easier to grow than cabbage and not easily destroyed by disease). The winged bean is also a very nutritious food crop. There are many staple foods grown in different parts of Papua New Guinea and people in each region have their own traditional way of growing these crops; for example, the Enga people grow kaukau in compost mounds and in Maprik and Drekkikir, the Sepik people grow very big yams by digging holes and filling them with leaves from the taun trees.

Although traditional crops are often the best, there are some good new crops such as corn, pineapple, beans, peanuts and fruit trees.

Before you plant a new crop you should ask the following questions:

- Will the seeds always be available?
- Will it cost money to buy seeds or can I produce my own?
- Will insects attack this crop?
- Will I need fertilisers to make these crops grow well?
- How nutritious is this food?
- Will I be able to sell excess stock at the market?

Mixed cropping

Mixed cropping is planting different types of crops in different parts of the same garden. This helps to prevent diseases and pests from spreading because they generally like only certain types of plants and will not spread to other plants in the garden. So, if you grow kaukau and it is affected by disease, the other plants such as corn, beans and peanuts will not be affected. Infected plants should be pulled out and burnt as soon as they are discovered.

Crop rotation

If you plant one crop, such as kaukau, in your garden and harvest it, you should plant a different crop, such as corn, in the same place after it. Then grow another different crop, such as beans, the next time around before growing kaukau again. This will help keep the soil fertile because different plants use different nutrients and some plants put nutrients back into the soil. It can also help stop many insects and diseases spreading.

Summary

- Plan your garden well.
- Do not burn everything when clearing a garden.
- Dig plants back into the soil after harvest.
- Make compost.
- Rotate crops.
- Use mulch to control pests and weeds.
- Plant mixtures of different crops in a garden.
- Burn diseased plants.
- Plant all year around.
- Store food correctly after harvesting and it will keep longer.

Planting methods

Common plant foods can be divided into three food groups.

- Staple energy foods: kaukau, cooking banana, cassava, taro, yams, sago, coconut, sugar cane
- Plant body-building foods: beans, peanuts, nuts
- Plant protective foods: green leaves, fruits

Traditional staple foods

Kaukau

Kaukau is a trailing vine that grows **tubers** under the ground. The tubers are an energy food containing starch and the young leaves can be eaten as a protective food.

Kaukau can be grown almost anywhere in Papua New Guinea, even in high altitudes, all year round. It requires little water and grows in most soils, but will produce best yields on sandy loam soils. It is usually grown in mounds or ridges.

Planting

- Use stem cuttings about 25-40cm long, taken from the youngest part of the vine.
- Stick half of the cutting into the soil with the other half sticking out.
- The planting hole should be 15-30cm deep.
- Cover mounds with soil and mulch during dry periods.

Care

- Weed two or three times before kaukau leaves completely cover the ground.

Kaukau continued ...

Harvest

- Harvest the roots three to seven months after planting, when the leaves turn yellow.

Use

- The roots can be eaten or used as stock feed.
- The leaves can be cooked with other green vegetables and are very rich in iron.

Cooking banana

Cooking bananas contain mostly starch although some of the starch turns to sugar in **ripe** fruit. Trees grow in large clumps and have bigger bunches of fruit than sweet bananas. They grow well on the coast and in the highlands to around 2000 metres. They prefer humid areas and do not like frosts.

Bananas can grow in a wide range of soils, as long as there is good drainage, fertility and moisture. They need plenty of compost and will not grow well in grass or weeds. They also need a lot of water, which can be a problem if there is a long dry season. Bananas are planted from suckers, which are the young plants that grow beside the mother plant, and will produce a bunch of fruit after one year. After that the tree dies and new suckers take its place.

Cooking banana continued ...

Planting

- Clear the land (do not burn).
- Dig holes at least 30cm deep and 30cm wide, deeper in soft sandy soil.
- Add a good supply of compost to the hole before planting the sucker.
- Plant 2m apart in rows about 4m apart.

Care

- The mother plant should be about six months old before a new sucker is allowed to grow – if any suckers come up before that, cut them out with a bush knife at ground level and dig out the centre of the remaining portion so that it will not grow again.
- Maintain only three suckers per plant all year round – one bearing stem, one smaller sucker and one young sucker – to produce big fruit.
- Plant a **cover crop**, such as cowpea, pumpkin or pineapple, and mulch to prevent weeds.

Harvest

- Harvest when the skins of the fruit are light green and shiny and have reached their full size.

Use

- Use the fresh fruit for eating and plantains for cooking.
- Dry and store or process into flour for cooking.
- The flowering tip can be used as a vegetable.
- The leaves are often used for wrapping food before or after cooking.

Cassava

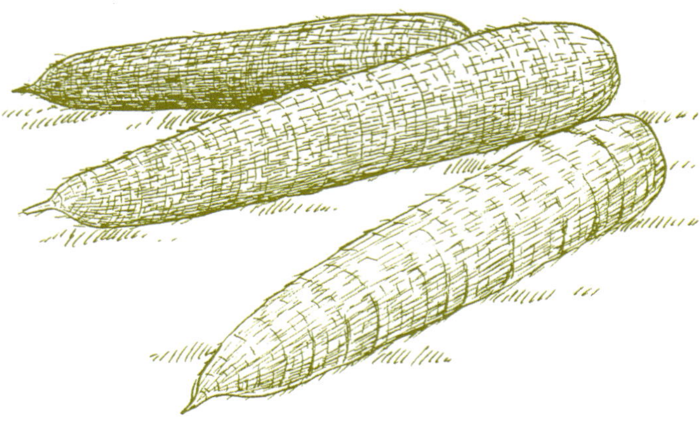

Cassava is a small scrub plant. It is common in many areas because it is pest-resistant and can produce good yields even in poor soils. It competes well with weeds and can tolerate dry weather. The tubers of cassava are an energy food containing starch. They are low in protein, but contain calcium, iron and vitamin C. The leaves of cassava are high in vitamin A and relatively high in protein, fibre, calcium and iron. The raw tubers (and leaves) also contain small amounts of poisonous chemicals, so they must be soaked in water for a long time to remove these substances before cooking.

Planting

- Push stem cuttings into the ground, about 1–1.5m apart.
- Stem cuttings should be 20–25cm long and 22–24cm thick with at least three buds.

Care

- Heap soil around the cuttings two to three months after planting to encourage tubers to form.

Harvest

- Harvest after nine months.
- Dig up a few tubers and try them when the leaves turn yellow and fall off.

Use

- The roots can be eaten and also used as stock feed.
- The green leaves are an excellent vegetable rich in vitamin A, protein, fibre, calcium and iron.

Taro

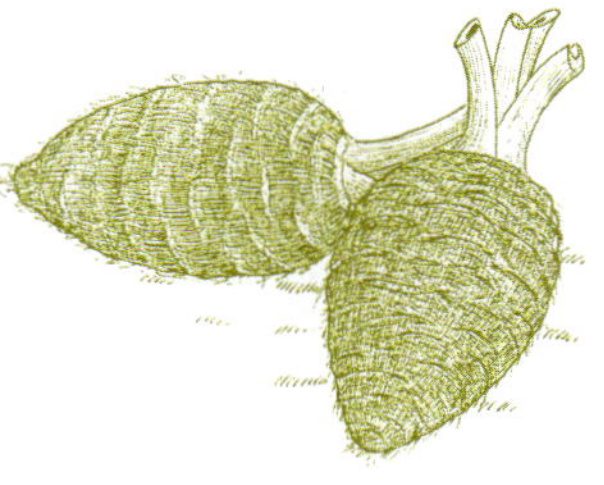

Taro is a plant that grows tubers. The underground tuber, or corm, is an energy food containing starch. The young leaves and leaf stems are protective food. Taro needs plenty of water to grow well and likes damp, shady places. Taro will grow in all kinds of soils but does best on dark, crumbly soil that is rich in organic matter.

Planting

- Use suckers (cormels around the plant) or the thick part of the stem under the ground, about 20cm in length (bigger plants will grow faster and give a higher yield).
- Plant stems or cormels in holes 10-20cm deep, 60cm apart, in rows 1m apart.
- Cover with 5-7cm of soil mixed with organic matter.
- Plant any time of the year shortly after the previous crop has been harvested.

Care

- Remove weeds and place mulch between suckers when taro plants are young.
- Heap up soil around the plant during the growing period to increase the yield.

Harvest

- Harvest when the leaves become smaller — five to six months after planting on the coast and up to 12 months in cooler areas.
- Dig up the corms carefully so that they are not bruised.
- Harvest during dry weather.

Note: *Taro corms can be stored in the ground until needed.*

Use

- Taro corms and cormels are an excellent energy food containing starch.
- The young leaves, including the stalks, are a good source of protective food.
- Cormels and leaves are also good stock feed.

Yams

The yam is a climbing vine. It forms underground tubers that contain starch and come in many shapes and sizes. The five different kinds of yams grown in Papua New Guinea are:

- greater yam
- lesser yam (esculenta)
- potato yam
- lesser yam (hispida)
- lesser yam (nummularia).

The potato yam grows tubers on the stem above the ground as well as under the ground and both kinds can be eaten. The tubers above the ground are sometimes poisonous so they should be washed and cooked thoroughly.

There is a large amount of work involved in growing yams so they are expensive to buy, but they have very high protein content and people should be encouraged to grow them. They are useful in times of food shortage because they keep well.

Yams like a hot and wet tropical climate with temperatures above 25 degrees and a minimum of 2150 millimetres rainfall annually. They like light and well-drained fertile soil and tend to rot in heavy clay soils.

In some places, particularly the Sepik and Trobriands, a great deal of work is put into preparing deep yam beds. These beds are built up from the ground and produce extremely large but low quality yams. Sometimes they are almost inedible but their size carries considerable prestige.

Yams continued ...

Planting

- Plant yams at the beginning of the rainy season.
- Plant in mounds about one or two metres apart.
- Use tuber cuttings of 500g, or small whole tubers when planting greater yam.
- For cuttings use the top of tubers which have been stored for a few months.
- Plant small whole tubers to get best results from the lesser yam.
- Plant in new gardens or rich well-drained soil.
- Make holes with a digging stick and put the tuber or little bulbs and pieces well into the soil.
- Add a stake or pole, about three to four metres high, next to each yam mound for the vine to grow on.

Care

- Keep yam plants free from weeds for at least three months.
- Add mulch and organic manure.
- Use crop rotation and disease-resistant varieties of yams.
- Destroy all diseased plant material.

Harvest

- Harvest when the vines start to die, about six to twelve months after planting.
- Delay harvesting for as long as possible to increase the yield.
- Only harvest yams as needed.

Note: *Yams can be stored in a well-ventilated yam house. Make sure they are free of soil and are not bruised during harvest.*

Use

- Tubers can be boiled, baked, fried, dried and made into flour.
- Yams store well in most coastal conditions.
- Peelings and waste can be used as stock feed.

Sago

Sago is a palm that grows about ten to 15 metres in the swampy lowlands. Sago starch is a very bulky food because it contains a lot of water. It is an energy food with almost no other value but it is difficult for people, especially children, to obtain enough energy to meet their daily requirements if they are only eating sago. There are two types of sago palms – one variety produces suckers and the other produces large seeds.

Planting

- Grow from suckers or seeds.
- Plant in the sunlight to produce a better yield.

Care

- Cut down tall trees near the sago palm.
- Cut away extra suckers when sago palms grow too close together.

Harvest

- Harvest sago when the trees are about 15 years old and hold the highest level of starch.
- Cut down the tree and split open the trunk.
- Beat or grate the pith to a pulp with a sago rasper.
- Wash the pulp and separate the water from the white sago starch.
- Wrap the sago in palm leaf bundles to preserve it.

Legumes

Many different kinds of beans grow easily in Papua New Guinea. Beans are important for their protein content, which is found in the seeds. Ripe seeds have much more protein than young green seeds. Bean plants produce quickly and can be used in many different ways. The leaves can be plucked for greens but this reduces pod production.

Cowpea

There are many varieties of cowpea. Black-eyed beans and china peas are grown for their dry seeds and yard-long beans, asparagus beans and snake beans are grown for the long immature pods. Cowpea is a hot weather crop and is fairly drought-resistant. It prefers temperatures of 20 to 35 degrees and altitudes up to 1500 metres. It will grow in a variety of soils, but cannot stand waterlogging.

Planting

- Plant seeds 10cm apart in rows up to 50cm apart.
- Don't plant during heavy rain or in highly fertile soil because leaf growth will dominate bean pod growth.

Care

- Control weeds in the early stages of growth.
- Use crop rotation.
- Destroy all diseased plant material.

Harvest

- Pick pods when they are golden brown.
- Pick pods early to avoid damage from insects and disease.
- Put them in copra bags and bash the bags on the ground to dry and thresh them.

Winged beans

There are many varieties of these beans and they are very useful because all parts of the plant are nutritious and can be eaten. The bean is eaten whole when it is green but once the seed ripens, only the seeds can be eaten. Winged beans can be grown in any type of well-drained soil in almost all parts of Papua New Guinea except for altitudes above 1800 metres.

Planting

- Plants seeds in holes about 20cm deep.
- After six to eight weeks, stakes should be provided between two to three plants.
- Stakes should be 2-3m high for a bean crop and 1-1.5m high for a tuber crop.

Care

- Control weeds for the first six weeks.
- Avoid heavy rainfall or over-watering.

Harvest

- Harvest flowers, leaves and green pods for eating after three months.
- Harvest roots after five to six months.

Peanut

Peanuts can be grown almost everywhere in Papua New Guinea but prefer areas with a dry season. When the plant produces flowers, the flower dies and leaves a small pod. This pushes down into the ground underneath the plant and grows until it matures for harvest.

The peanut's main value is protein. It is a useful food when eaten raw, but it is better when cooked (roasted or boiled) as our bodies can make better use of the protein. Peanuts contain a lot of fat, which is an energy food, and are also rich in vitamins B and E.

Planting

- Plant in ridges on light soil.
- Plant about 10cm apart in rows about 60-80cm apart.
- Plant loose seeds or seeds still in the pods (loose seeds give best results).

Care

- Control weeds in the early stages of growth.
- Hold branches down to the ground with small stones to produce high yields.

Harvest

- Harvest after three to five months, when the leaves start to turn yellow.
- Pull out the crop by hand and turn it over in the sun to dry before stripping the nuts.

Use

- Add peanuts to vegetable stews.
- Roast over a fire (shelled or unshelled) for 15 to 20 minutes.
- Cooked peanuts can be ground into flour and added to a baby's food.

Sugar cane

Sugar cane is grown from a stem cutting of an old sugar plant and needs fertile, well-composted soil. In the lowlands, sugar cane matures in 12 to 14 months but it may take up to two years to mature in the highlands. The stem of the sugar cane contains a large amount of energy food as well as sugar. It needs a period of dry weather to build up the sugar stores in the cane.

Planting

- Plant stem cuttings with two or three nodes about 1m apart.

Care

- Control weeds.

Harvest

- Cut the stems when they appear woody.
- Squeeze or eat within two days of cutting as the sugar content drops rapidly after that.

Use

- Crush stems to produce fresh juice for drinking and dark sugar for cooking.
- Use dried crushed stems to make fuel.

Coconut

The flesh of mature coconuts is mainly used to give flavour to other foods, but it is also a good energy food and contains fat. The water from young green coconuts is called kulau and it is a good source of vitamin B. Coconut palms need moist fertile soil and good pest control. Once established, a coconut palm can live 80 to 100 years.

Planting

- Grow from mature nuts.

Care

- Control pests.
- Use pesticides if necessary.
- Young trees may need barriers against rats.

Harvest

- Pick green coconuts from the tree (after careful climbing).
- Mature coconuts will fall to the ground.

Use

- Use kulau for drinking and cooking.

Traditional vegetables

There are many different kinds of nutritious green vegetables already growing in Papua New Guinea. Green leaves contain good amounts of vitamins B and C as well as two important minerals – iron and calcium. The following vegetables are easy to grow, very nutritious, produce big yields and relatively free from pests and diseases. General rules for growing greens are as follows:

- grow traditional green vegetables
- grow all year round
- grow many different types
- do not over-cook them.

Aibika

Aibika grows well in coastal areas and up to 1600 metres on any dark loose soil. The leaves and soft top stems are rich in vitamin C, calcium and iron.

Planting

- Plant stem cuttings or young stems from the tip after harvest.
- Dig rows 1m apart.
- Plant stem cuttings when it is raining or water the soil before planting.

Care

- Weeding is essential.
- Vulnerable to pests and diseases, including beetles that make holes in the leaves.

Harvest

- Harvest three to four months after planting.
- New leaves sprout after first harvest so this plant can be harvested more than once.

Use

- Sell or eat quickly after harvest as the leaves do not last long.

Aupa

This drought-resistant plant grows well even in poor soils as long as it is given nutrients, but will not tolerate frosts. It contains protein, vitamin A, calcium and iron.

Planting

- Plant seeds at least 30cm apart.

Care

- Disease-resistant but can be damaged by grubs chewing the leaves of the young plant.

Harvest

- Harvest first after four weeks by **thinning** the seedlings.
- Discard the roots but the leaves can be eaten.
- Harvest again when the plant is 6-8cm high.
- Pick the tops of the aupa and the sides will continue to grow so you may have a third harvest.
- After that, the plant will begin to dry up.

Use

- Cook straight away as leaves do not last long.

Karakap

Karakap is a small herb found in damp shady parts of most food gardens.

Planting

- Usually self-sown but can be scattered if necessary.

Care

- Disease-resistant but some damage from leaf-eating bugs can occur.

Harvest

- Harvest after three months but best before flowering.

Use

- The juices of karakap leaves are used to treat ringworm, gout and earache.
- Leaves can be cooked in coconut milk or mixed with tinned fish.
- The ripe berries (dark purple) are edible.

Lowland pitpit

Lowland pitpit is a cane with an edible flower. It grows in coastal areas, the lowlands and in altitudes up to 1800 metres. It grows well among weeds on **fallow land** and takes seven to nine months to flower, depending on the variety.

Planting

- Use stem cuttings 30-40cm long with three to four nodes, from a mature plant.
- Put three to four cuttings into deep holes, 12-14cm apart, with 20cm of the stem above the ground.

Care

- Needs little care but can be affected by insects.

Harvest

- Harvest when most of the leaves on the stalk are brownish and the leaf sheaths lose their hair.

Use

- The unopened flower at the top of the plant is edible.
- It can be eaten raw or cooked over an open fire or in coconut milk with other vegetables.

Highland pitpit

Highland pitpit is a hardy plant that can grow in dry or damp soil. It grows in many parts of Papua New Guinea, especially in areas above 2100 metres.

Planting

- Break off a side shoot and plant in newly prepared soil on the edge of ditches.

Care

- Needs little care but can be attacked by rust.

Harvest

- Harvest the big shoots after four to five months before leaves become too hard.
- Pick at the base of the leaves to encourage new growth.

Use

- Use the leaves as a leafy vegetable and the bark as fibre for bilums, baskets and grass skirts.

Kangkong

Kangkong grows wild in swamps, rivers and ponds but can be cultivated and grows quickly.

Planting

- Plant stem cuttings or throw them in a swampy area.

Care

- Needs little care but control weeds and other **parasites** that may hinder growth.

Harvest

- Harvest the tips.

Use

- The leaves and stems are soft and tasty when cooked in coconut cream and steamed or fried with meat.

Tulip

Tulip lives for a long time and grows almost everywhere in Papua New Guinea, especially the Sepik area. The young leaves and seeds are edible and have a nutty taste.

Planting

- Usually grown from seeds or young trees dug out of the forest.
- Plant seeds in seed beds and transplant young trees about 50cm high.
- Plant 4-5m apart as the trees grow tall and spread out.

Care

- Needs little care.

Harvest

- Harvest about two weeks after new leaves form but before they become too hard.
- Pick from the base of the leaves to encourage new growth.

Use

- Use the leaves as a leafy vegetable and the bark as fibre for bilums, baskets and grass skirts.

Kund

Kund is a traditional highland vegetable. The young green flowers contain seeds and turn brown when fully matured. It grows well in wet soil.

Planting

- Plant in a mixed garden when rain starts.
- Scatter seeds when the soil is wet.

Care

- Thin out plants during early growth so that a few plants can grow better.
- Young plants that are removed can be cooked and eaten.

Harvest

- Harvest mature tops before the flowers appear.

Use

- Gives a nice flavour in roast meat and chicken dishes.

Introduced vegetables

Introduced vegetables can grow in many regions of Papua New Guinea but are more susceptible to pests and diseases than traditional vegetables. They require rich soils with good nutrients. Many introduced vegetables are hard to grow, produce low yields and require time and money (for pesticides) until the crop is ready for harvest.

Corn

Corn (maize) grows well in both lowlands and highlands to 2500 metres. Corn grows on many soil types if there is good rainfall and drainage, but needs fertile soil and will not grow well on land that has been cropped for a number of years.

Planting

- Plant two seeds in each hole about 3-5cm deep and in rows 70cm apart.
- Do not plant another crop of corn directly after the first crop.

Care

- Control weeds during early growth.
- Remove the weakest plant from each hole.
- Plant another crop like legumes with the corn to keep the soil fertile.
- Can be attacked by rust, leaf blight, downy mildew and blister smut.
- Use crop rotation and disease-resistant varieties instead of expensive pesticides.

Harvest

- Harvest at different times depending on its use.
- Pick when nearly all the cobs are full size and yellow (three to five months depending on the region).

Use

- Leave cobs until they are fully ripe, hard and dry for making flour or stock feed.

Potato

Potato is a popular vegetable in the highlands. It grows best in a moderate climate with deep loose soils that are well composted and drained. Potato grows faster than kaukau, contains more protein and can keep longer.

Planting

- Plant healthy whole tubers or tuber cuts.
- Plant seeds 15cm deep after rain.
- Plant in mounds or long ridges, wide enough for two rows, to provide drainage.

Care

- Vulnerable to many pests especially potato tuber moth.
- Does not tolerate waterlogging.

Harvest

- Harvest after three to four months depending on altitude.
- Dig them up before all the leaves and stalks completely dry out.

Pumpkin

Pumpkin grows well in many soil types but prefers composted soil. Vines will continue to produce pumpkins for up to a year. The young leaves and seeds have a nutty taste.

Planting

- Plant any time of the year but germination may take longer in colder areas.

Care

- Mildew can sometimes be a problem.
- Lift ripening fruit clear of damp ground and support with dry grass or wood.
- Watering may be needed in dry areas.

Harvest

- Harvest the fruit after three to four months although green leaves and tips will be ready before this.
- Mature pumpkins often change colour where the fruit touches the ground.
- The stem shrivels slightly and there is a reduction in leaf growth.

Cabbage

Cabbage grows on the coast and in the highlands but prefers cooler areas. It is vulnerable to pests and diseases including diamond back moth, cutworm, downy mildew, leaf spot, soft rot, black rot and club root.

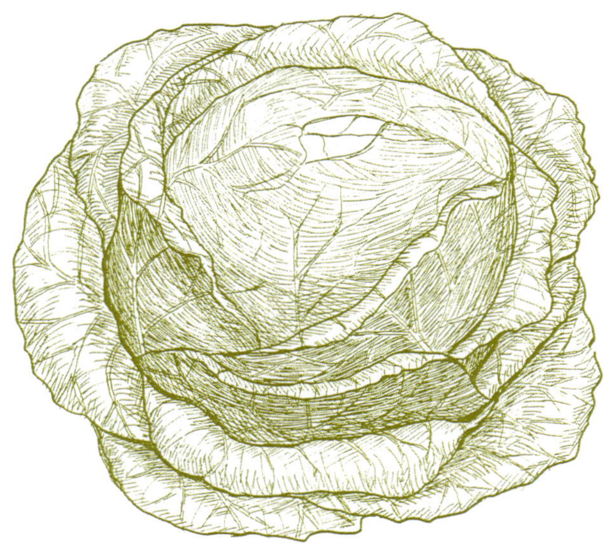

Planting

- Plant seeds in seed beds with two seeds in each hole and remove one if two grow.
- Transplant young seedlings at four to five weeks when they have three to four leaves.
- Plant young cabbages in rows about 50cm apart.

Care

- Control weeds.

Harvest

- Harvest after two months in coastal areas and three months in the highlands.
- Cabbage heads must be strong and tight – they will break and lose leaves if left in the garden too long.

Cucumber

Cucumber grows best in strong sunlight and temperatures of 18 to 24 degrees. It needs well-drained soil, rich in organic matter. It can grow on the ground or climb on a frame, which saves space and improves quality. Cucumber is vulnerable to fungal diseases on the leaves in humid areas.

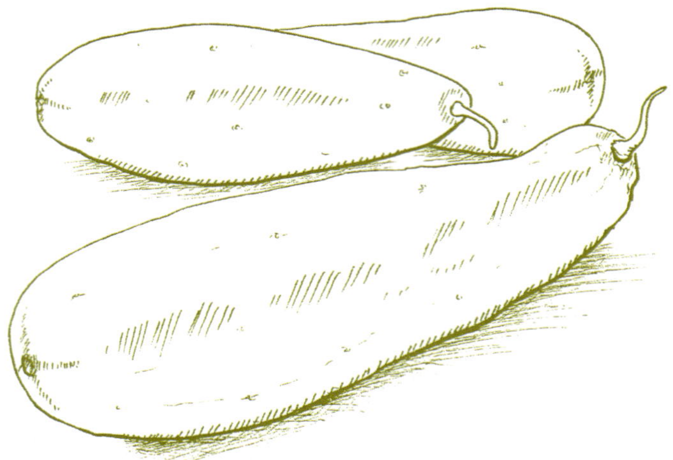

Planting

- Plant seeds in seed beds with two seeds in each hole and remove one if two grow.
- Transplant young seedlings in four weeks in rows 30cm apart.

Care

- Control weeds until the plant establishes itself and spreads.
- Lift ripening fruit clear of damp ground and support with dry grass or wood to prevent mildew.

Harvest

- Harvest fruit after three months.

Use

- Old fruit can be dried and used as seed.

Tomato

Tomatoes grow in rich moist soil in areas where it is warm during the day and cool at night, up to 1800 metres. Tomatoes are vulnerable to many soil-borne pests and diseases, especially during the rainy season.

Planting

- Plant seeds in seed beds and transplant after three to five weeks when young plants are 10-15cm high.
- Plant 40cm apart in a single row.

Care

- Control weeds.
- Put dry mulch under small tomatoes during dry periods.
- Remove any unhealthy leaves before watering.
- Tie plants loosely to stakes for support.

Harvest

- Harvest the fruit when it changes from green to red.
- Pick carefully by hand and carry in baskets.
- Do not stack fruit on top of each other.

Use

- Eat quickly as they do not keep well.

Fruit trees

Fruit is grown all over Papua New Guinea. Pawpaw, bananas and pineapple are very popular. Fruit trees provide shade as well as fruits that are rich in vitamins and minerals and can be eaten fresh, without cooking. There are many other delicious fruits like rambutan, mango and passionfruit that can be grown in villages.

Pawpaw

Pawpaw grows in well-drained, well-composted topsoil and is found on the coast and up to 1600 metres. It can be planted any time of year as long as water is available. The edible part of the pawpaw is a rich source of vitamin A and also has some vitamin C. Pawpaw trees can either be male or female or both. Male and female trees can be recognised by the shape of their flowers. It is occasionally attacked by fruit fly but is generally pest-free. Trees start to bear fruit after 12 to 18 months in the highlands and six to ten months in the lowlands. Trees may live for up to 25 years, but yield will decline with age.

Planting

- Plant seeds in holes 1cm deep and 10cm apart.
- Transplant seedlings from nursery beds when they are 15-20cm high, about 3-4m apart plant five or six seedlings in one hole and grow for six months.

Care

- Check the sex of the trees after they flower and remove all but one male tree for every nine female trees.

Harvest

- Harvest when the underside of the pawpaw skin begins to turn yellow (fruit will ripen in four to five days).

Pineapple

Pineapple grows well in the lowlands and in the highlands up to 1700 metres. There are two main varieties in Papua New Guinea: the rough leaf variety has spines on the leaves and produces sweet fruit, while the smooth leaf variety has spineless leaves and produces larger but less sweet fruit. Pineapple can be planted any time of the year provided it is not too dry. After the fruit has been harvested, the mother plant must be cut off and all but one of the suckers removed. Pineapples are relatively free of pests or diseases but can be attacked by mealy bug.

Planting

- Plant 30cm apart in rows 60cm apart or individually.
- Plant from the following:
  - ✓ tops or crown of a pineapple
  - ✓ slips – leafy branches that grow on the fruit stalk just below the fruit
  - ✓ aerial suckers – leafy branches that grow on the stem above ground level
  - ✓ ground suckers – leafy branches that grow up from the stem below ground level
  - ✓ butts – the stems of the plants that can be used for planting after the fruit has been harvested.

Care

- Cover the ground with mulch or waste material from other crops to control weeds.

Harvest

- Harvest after about one year.
- Plants grown from aerial suckers produce fruit first with butts taking the longest.
- The fruit turns yellow or orange when it is ripe.
- Heap soil around the base of the remaining sucker so that the roots can easily obtain food from the soil.

Passionfruit

This is a fast-growing wood climber, relatively free of pests and diseases, that will not grow in heavy or poorly-drained soils.

Planting

- Plant from ripe fruit without removing the pulp.
- Transplant seedlings after three to four months, about 3-7cm apart.

Care

- Provide trellises of posts and wire for the vines to climb.

Harvest

- Harvest when green fruit turns deep purple.

Mango

This hardy, evergreen tree lives for many years. Mango fruit are a good source of vitamin A and trees will continue to fruit for up to 40 years.

Planting

- Plant from fresh seeds in special seedbeds with an iron, stone or concrete floor to restrict the growth of deep tap roots.
- Seedlings can be planted 10-12m apart after the second group of leaves has formed.

Care

- Needs shade.

Harvest

- Harvest when fruit turns yellow to pink.

Guava

This is a shallow-rooted shrub or small tree that grows wild in some areas of Papua New Guinea. It is pest and disease-free, and the fruit is a great source of vitamin C and A as well as iron, calcium and phosphorous. Trees will continue to fruit for up to 30 years.

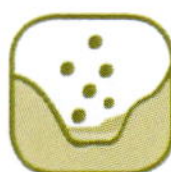

Planting

- Can be grown from seed.
- Seedlings should be transplanted 6-8m apart when they are 15-20cm high.

Care

- Needs little care.

Harvest

- Harvest fruit after one to two years.
- Green fruit turns light green or yellow and becomes soft when ripe.

Storing harvested food

- Do not leave harvested food in the sun. Heat and light can destroy many of the vitamins and minerals.
- Store food where there is plenty of fresh circulating air. Do not put it away in a hot box.
- Make sure that all the food is stored away from animals and pests such as pigs, dogs, chickens, rats, snakes and insects.
- If harvested food cannot be sold or used, preserve or dry it or make jam, peanut butter and so on.
- Put small amounts of food in clean containers such as tins, plastic bags or bottles. Store these in a cool shady place such as on a raised wooden or bamboo shelf. This stops food becoming damp and going bad and prevents insects eating it.
- Use the oldest food first. Do not store it until it goes soft and rotten and cannot be used.

Note: *If garden food is stored properly, it will keep well and can be used for a long period of time.*

Common storage methods

Fruit/vegetable	Storage method
Bananas	Generally bananas do not store well so should be harvested when they are needed; however, fruit harvested too early will not ripen well and will not taste good.
Yams	Yams will keep for several months if stored in a cool, dry, shady, airy place or in special yam houses.
Kaukau	Kaukau tubers store well in the ground, so can be dug up when they are needed. Kaukau will keep for two to three weeks if stored in a dark cool place and protected from insects.
Cassava	Most varieties of cassava can be left in the ground until needed. Although it will last a long time in dry weather, it becomes tough and bitter when left too long in the soil. After harvest, the tubers will only keep for three to four days.

Common storage methods continued ...

Fruit/vegetable	Storage method
Peanuts	Peanuts can easily be dried in the sun or over a fire by hanging them in their shells by their stalks. They can then be shelled and kept in clean airtight jars or made into peanut flour and stored. Peanuts are best cooked and eaten when freshly harvested.
Corn	If corn has been grown for eating it should not be stored but should be cooked soon after it has been picked, as it loses its sweetness very quickly after harvest. If it is to be used for planting it should be dried and stored in a cool airy place. Dried corn can also be ground into cornflour and kept in clean airtight jars.
Sago	Dry sago will keep well for up to six months if protected from insects and animals. It should be stored in clean airtight containers.
Potato	If potato tubers are dry, they can be stored in cool, dark, airy places for short periods of time, such as on wire shelves in a storehouse. The storehouse must be dark enough to prevent the potato from turning green.
Pumpkin	The fruit should be stored in a warm, dark, dry place. It will keep for many months but check regularly for signs of rot.
Pineapple	Pineapples do not keep well and should be eaten after harvest.
Pawpaw	The green fruit will keep for some time if kept cold and in the shade. The fruit can be picked green, allowed to ripen and then eaten immediately. Ripe fruit cannot be stored.
Guava	The fruit should be picked when ripe. It cannot be stored and should be eaten immediately after harvest.
Green beans	Beans will store for a few days in a cool shady place but they are better picked and eaten fresh.
Green leafy vegetables	Green leaves should be picked, cooked and eaten immediately. Some leaves will keep for a few days in a cool dark place but they will lose many of their nutrients over this time.

Selling food at the market

Preparing vegetables

Preparing vegetables for market is very important because it will determine the amount of money that you make. The better the quality of your vegetables, the higher price you can ask – poor quality produce will get a low price or may not sell at all.

Washing

Wash all the soil off root vegetables such as kaukau, yams, and potatoes. Dry them well to prevent rotting, especially if they are going to be stored or transported long distances.

Trimming

The presentation and appearance of vegetables is important. Remove all plant parts which are old, full of holes or diseased.

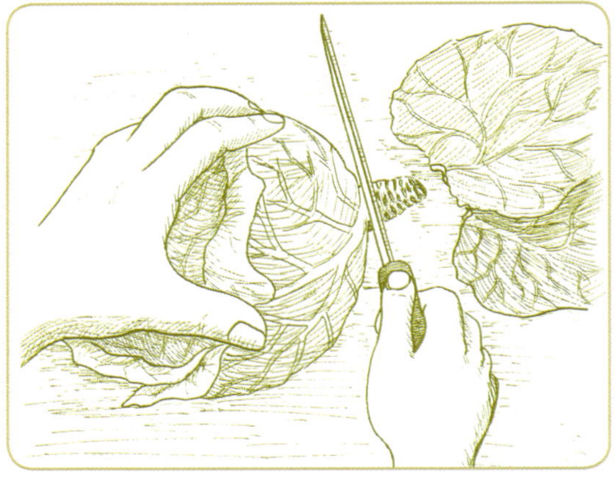

Grading

Group together all vegetables of the same size, shape, colour and quality and price accordingly.

Bunching

Leaves and stems should be tied together in bunches so that they look neat and tidy, and priced according to quality and quantity.

Packing

Soft vegetables like tomatoes must be packed in small strong baskets to avoid bruising. Other vegetables like kaukau and carrots may be packed in bags or piled up in baskets.

Traditional ways of bundling vegetables

Local farmers have traditional ways to bundle their vegetables for market. They have developed these skills over time and found them to be very effective.

Common bundling methods

Crop	Type of bundle	Quantity	Colour	Maturity
Beans	Very thin rope	12 pods	Green and fresh	Young
Tomatoes	Heap	6 fruits	Dark red and pink	Not over-ripe
Cabbage	Heap	6 heads	Green and fresh	Fresh leaves
Corn	Heap	6 cobs	Green and fresh	Seeds not too hard
Aibika (green)	Heap	2 tops	Dark green	Fresh leaves
Cucumber	Heap in sizes	6 fruits	Green and fresh	Young
Watermelon	Heap in sizes	6 fruits	Green and fresh	Not over-ripe
Banana	Heap in bunches	4 bunches	Yellowish	Almost ripe
Peanut	Heap in bunches	12 pods	Dark brown	Seeds not too soft

Transportation to market

Pack and load produce carefully so it is not damaged, or it might not sell. Soft vegetables need to be packaged carefully in suitable bags, baskets or containers so that they don't bruise. Get produce to market quickly. Some produce like greens needs to be harvested and brought to market on the same day if possible.

Market price

Market price is the price buyers are willing to pay for produce. If there is a lot of the same vegetable at the market, the price of this vegetable will be low as the supply is greater than the demand. If there is less of another vegetable, then the price will be high because the supply is scarce.

It is to the advantage of every farmer to harvest produce and sell it in the market when it is still scarce, as the price will be high. Once every farmer brings the same product to market and the supply becomes plentiful, the price will drop lower as supply exceeds demand.

Prices fluctuate during market day. Most farmers don't like to carry their produce back home as transport costs are high, so they will reduce the prices of unsold produce during the afternoon. However, good quality produce at reasonable prices will usually sell quickly and there will be no need to reduce prices for unsold stock.

At every market, no matter how small:

- there are sellers who offer produce for sale
- there are buyers who want produce and have the money to buy it
- prices are determined by the amount of produce supplied by the sellers and the demand of buyers
- prices are determined by the quality of the produce on offer.

Financial management

A budget is a statement of:

- how much money will be spent on what
- how much income is expected and when.

A farm budget should include:

- what and how much to grow
- what resources are required to grow crops
- what and how much will be sold
- what will be the income from the sale.

Note: *If the income (money from sales) is higher than the cost (expenses) you will make a profit.*

Planning a budget

Budgeting is part of planning a food garden. You need to collect information such as the price of seed, fertiliser and tools so you can start to prepare a budget. It's important to write your budget and plans down. Keep records in writing so you will know exactly how much money was spent to produce vegetables, how much money was made selling them, and whether you made a profit.

To be a successful farmer and run a profit-making business, no matter how small, you need to keep an accurate journal and financial records. The production journal should include growth and production information, which is basically everything that happened while growing the crops. Financial records should include all matters relating to expenses and revenue. It is important to keep records of how much it costs you to grow your produce and how much revenue you receive for it. It is best to keep a simple financial record for each crop you cultivate.

Sample farming journal

June 2007	Crops: kaukau, corn, potato
Monday	*Prepared mounds for kaukau planting* *Corn planted in plot 1*
Tuesday	*Planted kaukau in mounds*
Wednesday	*Spread compost over plot 2*
Thursday	*Prepared soil in plot 3 for planting of potato*
Friday	*Checked for pests in all plots – none seen*
Saturday	*Mended fences, weeding*

Sample financial record

Production costs

Date	Item	Cost
20 March	1 bag of fertiliser	K24
25 March	cucumber seed	K5

March 2007: total costs K29

Harvest revenue

Date	Vegetable	Quantity harvested	Value – sold at market
March 30	Cabbages	20 @ K1.8	K36
	Tomatoes	4kg @ K2.5	K10
	Aibika	10 toea per bunch	K5

March 2007: total revenue: K51

Summary: March 2007

Total revenue	K51
Total costs	K29
Profit/loss	**K22 profit**

Glossary

bacteria (singular: bacterium)	micro-organisms that can cause plant and animal diseases
compost	rotting plant and animal matter that can be used to add nutrients to soil
corm	the tuber of a plant
cover crop	a plant from the legume family, planted to cover the soil while the land is not planted
cultivate	dig the soil to loosen it so that water can soak into it and grow crops
decomposition	when plant and animal matter breaks down into compost and humus
disease organism	any living thing that causes sickness in plants and animals
drainage	removal of excess water from a piece of land
erosion	wearing away of the soil surface by running water, wind, or ice
fallow land	a piece of land that is left unused for some years before it is planted again
fertile	rich in nutrients
fertiliser	substances that can be mixed with soil to add nutrients
fungi (singular: fungus)	a simple plant or micro-organism that causes sickness and diseases in other plants
humus	part of the soil made from rotten plant material
loam	a rich type of soil made up of sand, silt and clay that is best for planting most crops
manure	animal dung from chickens, pigs, or cattle added to a garden to enrich the soil
mildew	disease that produces a white powdery growth on plants
mound	soil collected into circular raised heaps, commonly used for planting yams, tapioca, sweet potato and other crops

mulch	dried leaves and grasses placed around the base of a plant to reduce water loss and soil temperature, control weeds and add plant food to the soil
nutrients	any element that an animal, plant or human takes in and uses to grow such as nitrogen, potassium and phosphorus
organic matter	decayed remains of plants and animals, added to the soil to enrich it
organism	a living plant or animal of any size
parasite	a plant or animal that lives off other plants and animals, sometimes causing sickness or hindering growth
ridge	a long continuous seedbed with a triangular cross-section and a base of 30-45cm
ripe	fully mature and ready for eating or cooking
root	part of a plant, usually found under the soil, that absorbs water and nutrients from the soil and also anchors the plant to the soil
seed	a small structure usually found inside a fruit and which can grow into a new plant
seed bed	a square or rectangular area (or box) used for planting seeds and taking care of the seedlings before they are transplanted in the garden
seedling	a young plant that has grown out of seeds
spade	a hand tool with a flat blade used for digging holes
spore	a tiny particle of fungus
stem	part of a plant that bears leaves, branches and buds from which new plants can grow
storage	keeping or preserving farm produce for later use or sale
thinning	to pull out seedlings for good spacing, water and food from the soil

topsoil the surface layer of the soil, just a few millimetres thick, usually dark in colour and rich in plant nutrients

transplant to transfer a young plant from where it was initially grown to a permanent place in the garden

tuber a plant such as tapioca whose roots are swollen with stored food materials

virus a micro-organism that lives on plants or animals and can cause serious diseases

vitamins natural substances in food, necessary for the normal growth and function of a human or animal

weed any plant that grows where it was not planted and competes with crops for food, sunlight, and water

yield the amount of food produced

Notes

Notes *continued ...*

Notes *continued ...*

Notes *continued ...*

Notes *continued* ...